Sales

Mastering The Art Of Selling

10 Mistakes To Avoid Like The
Plague, 12 Powerful Techniques To
Reveal Any Hidden Objections &
Close The Sale

By Adam Richards

Table of Contents

Introduction

We are always selling something every day, be it trying to sell our services when going for an interview or during a garage sale. While we are always selling something, how can you make the difference and be that salesperson that can always make a sale each time they speak to a customer? Before you can learn about all the techniques you need to have to be a successful salesperson, it is also advisable to practice a few ethics.

The key to being a successful sales person is to be in a position to convince someone to buy without any tricks. I mean, by the time you are done talking to a potential customer, they are supposed to simply think that they can't leave without what you are selling; that's when you will know that you can sell anything.

What most sales people don't understand is that sales is not about manipulating but rather about your art of persuasion. If you are relying on manipulation, then you have it all wrong because while you can fool many people most of the time, you cannot fool everyone all the time so your days are numbered as people will eventually see right through your manipulation. The art of persuasion is what is going to get you over the top. So, what is the difference between manipulation and persuasion?

While persuasion relies on truly convincing someone that a certain purchase will benefit them, manipulation relies on using tricks in order to make a sale.

You should also not use puffery if you want to be a successful sales person. Puffery simply refers to expanding the truth beyond a certain line. If you are good, persuasion is all that you need to be the best sales person; no need for tricks. As you attempt to make a sale, you need to avoid lying since once a consumer realizes that you lied, that is basically the end of you.

Trust me; any costumer who has been conned into buying something that was a total opposite of what you told them will definitely not be the smiling type. While lying may make you make a sale now, your lies will be uncovered and when that time comes, you may be out of the job.

Most important of all, if a customer asks you about a question and you don't know the answer just be honest rather than saying something that does not make sense. You will be amazed that a customer will appreciate your honesty. Furthermore, customers are likely to buy products and services from sales people who look honest.

Now that you know a few things that you can do and those that you cannot do if you want to be a successful sales person, let us discuss how you will be able to reach a point where you can sell anything.

Chapter 1:

The Inner Game Of Sales:

How To Sell Without Losing

Your Soul

Selling constitutes the gist of all kinds of businesses. Though we often sell our point of views, professional selling involves selling of tangible or intangible products that may not be as simple as it may sound. Ask yourself a question – Would you buy something that you don't really need without giving it a second thought? Probably not; this is why if you want to be a successful sales person, you need to learn how to persuade and convince your prospects.

The Inner Game of Sales

Selling isn't merely about making the prospective buyer buy what he wants or what you may offer. It is also about making the buyer buy your perception about that service or product and start seeing it the way you have projected it. Selling is a mind game that needs to be first understood and then practiced. It relies on your belief that remains rested in your conscious as well as subconscious mind.

If we carry some sturdy opinion about the product or the service, and our mind believes in it, our selling power will get auto-empowered. For you to excel in sales, you ought to get a hold of your thoughts, ideas, and levels of concentration. Collect your mind and its ideas and pour it out in the form of conviction. This would set you on the right track and selling will start coming to you naturally.

Two important ingredients that would ensure you are making sales are *positive attitude* and *prompt actions*. Any delay in thinking or executing your plan would spoil the game.

Some strategic tips are:

There isn't any definite sales strategy that would become a benchmark for all.

Sales' skills need consistent honing for better results

The salesperson has to be smarter and rapt than the buyer to make him buy

Keep on innovating your strategies to not just sell your product but also prove it

Garner enough willingness, focus and concentration to excel in selling

How To Sell Without Losing Your Soul

Being a salesperson isn't easy. Even more difficult is to be an ethical salesperson who would sell without losing his or her soul. No one would believe a fake salesperson that puts on the charade of knowing you the moment they meet you. You would be shocked to know how the modern buyer is smart and knowledgeable.

So, instead of using your fake demeanor to sell, resort to some genuine counseling of your customer's need and sell the product out of his willingness. Believe in establishing a mutual and cordial relationship with your buyer without imposing yourself.

Here are some ways to be a likeable salesperson who believes in sane and rationale selling unlike those pushy ones who have gone redundant:

#1 Let Selling be not just Selling; solve a problem

The buyers are smart enough to gauge your mindset. They can sense if it is tilted towards hardcore selling or genuine for earning their loyalties. You don't have to focus on the word selling. Rather, take yourself as a guide who is going to help people in finding what they precisely need. This way, you would be able to understand the needs of your customers and appeal to their preferences.

#2 Do not be hell bent on selling

The harder you are trying to sell, the farther will your buyers be, out of distrust and doubt. Let the whole process of selling and buying be forgotten and lay stress on how you can help the customers. Trust me, it is going to show in your body language and you would end up being in the trusted books of your buyers. This would consequently help you in recommending your own product or service and customers will believe you easily.

If you want to be a successful sales person, you need to be honest and as natural as possible when trying to make a sale.

#3 Start slow and steady

As a salesperson, you may be a smooth talker. Talks and reasons may come to you effortlessly and you enjoy narrating them. However, selling is not all about ranting about what we know.

On meeting a prospective buyer, DO NOT even mention what you are selling during the first ten minutes. If you want to start talking about your product, prospective buyers will simply shut you out and no matter what you say, they are not going to buy anything.

Ideally, let your customers speak and listen carefully to know what they want. Your initial silence will go a long way in making the customer feel that you are really interested in helping them out if you can hear them out.

#4 Express instead of impress

Instead of impressing your customers be expressive and derive the same out of them. Do not use too much sales jargon such that they have to interpret your sales data. Rather, keep your selling approach simple and effortless. Shun the belief that buyers make their mind after watching glossy or flashy presentation. Rather, it makes them distracted from the real profile of the product.

#5 Create an irresistible offer

There are plenty of products or services out for sale on various platforms. To make your product outstanding, you have to offer what others haven't or cannot. If a product is sold for $200 and you are selling it for $200 only, no rampage would take place. Try selling the same product for just $199 and you will be amazed at how people can do everything to save even that $1.

#6 Take after-sale responsibility

Most of salespersons are usually just quick to sell you a product without even taking after-sales responsibility. This is a clear demarcation between a good and a bad salesperson. In order to carry on ethical selling, one simply cannot remain alienated from what happens to the product or service after the selling point.

Selling should include a satisfying experience that would come if the seller guides the buyers over after-sale problems. There needs to be effective interaction via feedback forms so that customers can give their feedback or ask for after-sales service.

#7 Guarantee quality or money back

One simple way to sell without losing your soul is to either deliver quality or return a customer's hard earned money. The money-back policy works like a charm, as the customer decides to try without any pitfalls for him.

A smart seller would not just sell a product but also rather sell the end result that would endorse their product even further. Buyers will then get comfortable and fearless in buying.

#8 Sell without being devious

Selling without any devious methods helps in building long term bonds. Once buyers are convinced about getting quality products or services from you, they will definitely become loyal customers. Don't just concentrate on 'selling'. Make your selling a worthwhile opportunity that will empower the buyer with a quality product.

For example, you have with you a costly silk carpet with intricate embroidery. In a city, it would be priced for more than several thousand dollars. Now you took it to countryside and sold it for $200 worth of terracotta pots. The potter may feel happy to get such an exotic carpet. Actually, this deal is completely absurd and futile, since the carpet has no or little value to the potter and is likely to remain hidden in their storage area. As a salesperson, you do not qualify as making an ethical or sensible deal.

Let us rewind the situation and assume that you gave an automated potter's wheel worth $100 to that potter in exchange of his terracotta pots. Now, this would be a sensible deal for the potter, as that automated wheel will help him in making many more pots in the future. He would be able to obtain a lot more value from the product you sold him for many years to come.

Consider all possibilities

The very fact that you have a brilliant idea does in no way imply that you are 'sorted' when it comes to being on the path to entrepreneurial success. You have to understand that there will be a lot of hurdles along the way, which could indeed lead to a lot of disappointment should things go askew in the process of setting up that business.

Of course you need to be mentally prepared for the same; the last thing you want is to be discouraged by the potential hurdles that come along your path, to the point where you want to throw it all away.

By being apprised of the hurdles that might come along, you are preparing yourself to be a lot more resilient than you otherwise would have been, thus paving the way for you to face any obstacle that might come your way. In fact, some of the most successful entrepreneurs out there are those that have embraced failure time and again, simply because they believed to the core in the ideas that they felt would change the world.

Of course it is vital that you have a great business idea to begin with. Sometimes you might just get that 'Eureka!' moment when you're sitting in a mall and observing things around you. But in addition to the pointers that we have discussed, one also needs to do a thorough amount of research into the idea that they have stumbled upon, in order to assess its viability in the market out there. The following chapter is an endeavor in just that. Let's take a look!

Chapter 2:

10 Characteristics Of Highly Successful Salespeople – Do You Have Any Of Those?

Selling cannot take place on its own. It always needs a salesperson that would make it a good or a bad sale. Effective and successful salespersons aren't trained in a day. They hone their skills out of experience and their innate study of customers' tendencies. Here are 10 characteristics that would make you a winning salesperson. Find out how many of these you possess.

#1 Determined

A great deal of persistence and determination is needed to be a good salesperson. There would be plenty of instances where you might have to face severe criticism or rejection. During such times, only determination will keep you afloat.

It is not easy to convince someone to buy anything even if it just costs a few dollars. It certainly takes a persevering mindset.

If you want to be a high achiever, don't just give up easily. A good sales person will not just take no for an answer and will be amazing at ensuring that at the end of the negotiations, the customer is convinced that they need to have what is for sale.

#2 Goal Setters

Nothing works without an aim or goal. Expert salespersons devise short as well as long term goals to meet success. They have clarity over what they want and work strategically towards it. They remain focused towards their goals and work against time to meet them. Ask any good salesperson to show his professional planner and you would see each hour of the day and every day of the week being preplanned to meet certain targets.

Each time you are talking with a prospective buyer, you should have a goal in mind, as this will even give you the motivation to convince the buyer that they need to buy what you are selling.

#3 Inquisitive

A good salesperson always has questions running through their minds. They remain aware and ask prospective customers intelligent questions. They ask questions to know more about the customer's needs so that they can know how their products and services come into the picture. They are also smart enough to endorse their products through their inquisitiveness.

#4 Good listeners

Successful salespersons are good listeners. They don't believe in using their own gab to sell their products. Rather, they gently persuade their customers to speak about their needs and then present their products or services in the same light. They first listen carefully and then summarize their selling stance.

If you want customers to buy from you, you need to listen to them so that you can know what their needs are and thus be better placed to show the customer how your product comes into place.

I would personally not want to buy anything from someone who just bombards me with the different benefits of a particular product or service without knowing whether I am interested in those benefits in the first place.

#5 Passionate

Being passionate is crucial if you want to be a successful salesperson. You have to be passionate about the product or else your selling will remain hollow and bleak. Good salespersons remain ever in love with their products and this increases their chances of selling effectively. Their every argument will be convincing enough and will exude their passion.

#6 Go-Getters

Successful salespersons cannot afford to be laid back otherwise; they would miss the leads and lose their contacts. They have to be always in close contact with potential buyers' base even on a personal level. Apart from the sales pitch, they remain in touch with the customers to find out how the products they bought are functioning as they should or they are experiencing any challenges. They follow up to know if the services the customer bought are suitable or not. They even call customers to know if they require certain products and services that they may have bought a while back.

A good salesperson will not sit and wait for the customer to ask about a particular product but will send reminders as well as more information about current products and services as well as new product and services being launched so that the customer can know what to expect.

#7 Confident

If you want to be the best salesperson, you have to be confident, persuasive and self-assured as rejection is a common feature here. Successful salespeople must not lose their heart after hearing a 'no'. Rather, they should be able to convert 'no', 'if' or 'but' into the affirmative like the true challengers they are.

#8 Patient

Successful salespersons do not rush into any deal, as they know how suicidal that can be. They handle their customers patiently and do not throttle them with their non-stop chatter.

Impatient salespersons would not do justice to their profile for they would not be able to feel the pulse of the market and their customers.

#9 Adaptable

Successful salespersons are flexible and adaptive to deal with all kinds of situations and customers. If nothing is working, they quickly alter their strategy and shift the pivot. The trick is to sell whatever you are selling in a language that the prospective customer understands.

#10 Show Empathy

Empathy is simply the ability to identify with customers to feel what they may be feeling and thus make them feel respected. You need to empathize with a customer and the challenges that they may be facing; hence, their need for your product. Once you can identify what they may be feeling, it is very easy to put your product or service in a way that the customer can buy such a product.

Additionally, a salesperson that is able to empathize with customers is likely to gain trust and build rapport with customers, which is crucial if you want to always be making a sale.

Chapter 3:

How Asking Questions Can

Increase Your Effectiveness

In the previous chapter, we saw how it is important for a salesperson to be inquisitive. The general notion goes like; customers ask innumerable questions to salespersons to know what are they selling.

However, the experts reiterate that salespersons should ask questions in order to first understand the needs of their customers and then to meet their sales target. You need to develop courage and acumen to ask questions without getting off-track.

How Asking Helps Selling

There is nothing offending or probing in posing questions to your customers as long as you are not asking offensive questions. On the contrary, it is appreciable for it leads to better understanding that consequently leads to customers' satisfaction.

Varied questions bridge the gap between the buyer and seller and solidify their mutual trust. There is also an element of personal bonding that is developed for better association.

Asking also helps by:

Uncovering painful points of customers for better negotiation

Initiating effective closure of sales

Confirming if prospect is genuinely interested in sales' lead

Finding the pulse of the customer

Fine tuning your sales pitch to make it customer-centric

Filtering the customers' information that would help you in selling

What to Ask

The questions listed below may not befit every prospect, but would give a fair idea on what to ask, and what not. These questions would also act as prompts and triggers for making prospects come out with their preferences.

HOT Questions

These refer to high order thinking questions that would put prospects on thinking spree. This will have a cascading effect over their issues, fears, pains, needs and requirements that would be addressed by introducing them the right product or service. These questions may be probing but need to be asked for clarity.

Clarifying Questions

There are times when prospects give vague and confusing information. In such cases, clarifying questions must be asked like – "Can you please elaborate further?"; "Tell me something more"; or "What do you want to convey?"

Feedback Questions

It is imperative to ask feedback questions for better insight and further improvement in the sales.

Prompt Questions

Be precise while negotiating. If no outcome is on the anvil, ask for next appointment without any hesitation.

This will leave a good impression over prospect. Ask questions like, "When can we meet next?"; "Would it be possible to meet next week?"; "How about meeting once again for further discussion"?

Questions for seeking commitment

If prospect fixes a time, do not hesitate to confirm. Make your prospect commit to you without feeling sheepish. Ask questions like – "Kindly confirm time". You can request prospects to include your call in schedule so that there can be no delay.

Sale Questions

After the entire conversation, don't forget to ask for the sale as an ultimate question. Ask specific questions like – "May I have your order please?" or "Can I expect to do business with you?"

Referral Questions

Referral questions carry the potential of fetching you further business via interpersonal networking. These questions have to be posed with confidence. Ask questions like, "Would you please refer someone from your professional circle?"

Chapter 4:

The 10 Biggest Mistakes Salesmen Usually Make - And How To Avoid Them

Before you can be that successful salesperson, you will definitely make many mistakes.

We will look at the 10 biggest mistakes that many salespeople make and the different ways to avoid them so that you do not make the same mistakes.

1. Talking more than listening

One of the most common mistakes committed by salespersons is talking more than they ought to listen. There is no point talking endlessly in front of the prospects and giving them no chance to state their needs and preferences. Ideally, a prospect should be doing nearly 70 percent of the talking.

Avoid this by being a patient listener, as it will help in gathering a lot of information that will definitely be helpful in enabling you make your sales pitch customer oriented. Listening does not only refer to listening to your prospects' words, but also through their body language.

For instance, if a prospect folds their arms, they may not be ready to open up to you so you had better ask suitable questions that will help them open up about their needs and what they expect of a product.

2. Vaguely Presuming

There is no room for vague assumptions in the sales business. Either you know what prospect wants or you don't. Making assumptions can be really harmful for they might backfire on you and you end up looking like a fool who doesn't seem to know what they are selling. You need to understand your prospect, their needs and then make an offer.

Avoid this by being a patient listener and take note of every point the prospect brings up.

3. Getting Defensive

Many salespersons become defensive when confronted by prospects, especially over price issues. Getting defensive and becoming apologetic shows your weakness and would affect the sale's pitch. The prospect will instantly capture your defensiveness through your body language and speech. Such situations should be handled with confidence and promptness. Do not jump to cut the rates simply on mere mention by the prospect.

Avoid this by stating the amazing features of your products or services that would justify your price bracket and make the customer see that they are getting value for their money.

4. Failing to make the prospect reveal their budget

Knowing the budget of the prospect can give you vital insight. Usually, salespersons do not work towards this. Knowing this area would help them in grabbing the deal easily, as you know how to state the product or service price and how farther the buyer can go.

Sometimes the buyer is usually willing to pay more for a certain product and once you state the price beforehand, you may not get the maximum amount of money from the customer. Try to get the prospect's budget before making any decisions.

Avoid this mistake by asking relevant questions that would make the prospect open up and reveal their needs and the budget threshold they are working with.

5. Excessive Follow Up

Excessive follow up, on phone or in person, can annoy the prospect and reverse the impact. Too much of chasing of prospective clients appears to be a stubborn behavior that sometime is taken in a bad taste.

A customer can easily change their mind and not buy the product when you are all over them and don't even give them time to evaluate their options and make a decision.

Avoid this by making your follow up brief yet effective. Gather enough information and work over it by staying in the background. Call up only when needed without sounding annoying.

6. Not taking time to build rapport

Being a salesperson requires social skills and establishing rapport with your prospect. It would be wrong to start discussing the sale too early or too late. Rather, build an understanding first and then steer towards sales. The absence of a mental connection between the buyer and seller will be first felt by your prospect only, making him reserved in his demeanor.

Avoid this by establishing a mental compatibility with your prospect so that he reveres and believes whatever you say.

7. Coming off as pleading

You are not pleading your customer to buy a product; your work is to persuade them. Your customer should come to a point that they see that they would derive great value from the product. If you come off as though you are pleading a customer to make a sale, you will come off as petty and rather if the customer were to make a purchase, they may be doing that so that you could just stop begging. You need to understand that you are offering a product or service that a customer will be happy to have.

Avoid this by sounding like a professional, who has potential to find solution to prospects' needs. This would earn you self-respect making you feel good.

8. Following a haphazard work approach

Following a chaotic work approach does not allow you to achieve your sales goals. Though it is good to be spontaneous and natural in pursuing your sales lead, being disorganized will make things very jumbled. Ensure you have an approach on how you plan to pursue a prospect. This however does not mean that you remain inflexible and not change according to your prospects' needs.

Avoid this by doing your homework well in advance to have an insight into your prospects' needs, followed by a systematic and methodical approach of achieving a sale.

9. Sounding and acting like competitors

If you are going to sound and act like other salespeople, how would your prospect distinguish and make a decision.

Being original and authentic will help you in having a different personality from the rest and you are likely to impress the prospect. This will also help in surpassing the competition.

Avoid this by equipping yourself with convincing facts and figures that would elevate the status of your product, leaving no reason to imitate others.

10. Zero prospecting

Prospecting is an integral part of selling. If this is not being done, a lot is being missed. Many salespersons keep on working over months old clients' list without adding or updating the same. This is like taking a circular track and reaching nowhere.

Avoid this by prospecting effectively through referrals, social media, friends, colleagues, cold calling, one-to-one interactions etc.

Chapter 5:

12 Sales Techniques For Revealing Hidden Objections – And How To Handle Them

Identifying the Veiled Objections

Interestingly, prospects often hide the truth from salespersons. Only few people would straightaway say

'No' to a proposal or come out directly with their objections. Now, the onus comes to the salesperson to identify the objections and actual reasons of rejections that have been simmering in the minds of customers.

Once a prospect starts evading meeting you and keeps on giving silly excuses, it is time to realize that objections have started developing. If you have tried to overcome initial hiccups and still the customer is relentlessly driving you nuts, maybe they are not telling you the real objection and are trying to dissuade you this way. Start reading their mind and body language to gather behavioral and contextual clues.

Contemplating the prospects psychologically will enable you to know the real objections. Probably it could be that they do not hold your products in very high regard or maybe your selling isn't impactful enough to shatter the barriers. Contemplate various reasons that may be bothering the prospect ranging from price to quality. If still nothing can be construed, talk to the prospect directly and be politely firm in asking the reasons for their doubts. Your rapport with your prospect will come in handy here. Offer to help them find a solution so that they can begin to trust you and open up.

Use your acumen to find the root cause of the objections. You could also study their pattern since that may give you some clue. Ask plenty of open-ended questions without forcing, to let them divulge what may be going on in their mind. Finding objections would be like a game of cards where you have to read the expressions expertly and come to a precise explanation.

Always be aware that customers don't always tell you the real objection. Always ask many open-ended questions. Always try to read the customer's facial expressions and body language. Always be confident enough to ask the customer the tough questions.

If you do these three things, finding hidden objections will become much easier for you.

Overcoming Objections

What your prospect may be saying to your face may not be the real objection. Once you have played the scrabble of their excuses, and unlocked the mystery, it is time to overcome them. Here are 12 excellent suggestions that would help you in identifying objections and successfully dealing with these objections in order to ensure a successful closure of a business deal:

#1 - For starters, do not be quick to respond. Rather, prod your prospect to talk at length over what may be bothering them. Gentle prodding will let you know the prime reason of their objection. Through that, you get to identify the real issue from its root cause. While the prospect is talking at length about their issue, you will get enough time to think about how to respond.

#2 - To keep price related objections at bay, don't mention price during early stages of the conversation. First, try to get the prospect capture the true worth of the product so that pricing will not bother later, as early mentioning of price results in loss of grip over prospects' articulation, and converts discussions to negotiations.

#3 - One best way to resolve most of the objections is to focus not on the product but on its worth. For example, if you want to sell an air-frying appliance, sell the idea of saving health by eating oil-free food.

Meeting objections is a clear indication that you haven't projected the value of product in the right way. Touch down the prospects' needs and goals to articulate them accordingly.

#4 - Keep calm and slow down your reactions. Acting in haste or on impulse will not resolve any issue. Do not let your emotions take over your common sense. Invest some quality time and thought to push the sale constructively. The prospect may try to make you jittery, but don't give in to this psychological trap.

#5 - Many people take shield of phony objections to negotiate. Get the right picture and identify what exactly is running through their mind. If negotiations are solicited, then steer your selling strategy accordingly. Find the right motive and address it.

#6 - Ask the prospect if resolving the issue will help in taking things further or not. This will help you in checking the authenticity of the prospect's intention to remain involved in the discussion. If objections are genuine and addressable, alter the package to bridge the gap.

#7 - If need arises, restructure the deal and offer what the prospect wants. Subtract or substitute value to meet the mutual objectives midway. However, do not make any compromises over quality or else, your reputation may suffer.

#8 - Ask some intelligent questions that would put the prospect in rethinking mode. Project your product or service smartly to let the prospect think what they may be missing.

#9 - Turn the table by arguing from buyer's point of view. If quality is the issue, reiterate the point of quality stating that's what differentiates your product.

It would be like singing the tunes of your prospect so that they understand it better. Use your expertise to invalidate maneuver objections into your favor.

#10 - Evoke emotions and empathy to stir prospect's response. This would work where quality is in question. Making statements like – "We compete for quality and not price" could make the prospect think twice.

#11 - Extend reassurance to the prospect vouching for your product or service. Furbish reference and testimonials to authenticate your claim and to thaw out objections. If prospect is still hesitant over price, assure them of greater value.

#12 - One effective way of dealing with objections is to make them taste their own medicines. If they are dilly-dallying with deals, catch them off guard by saying "Take some time to think and reconsider the offer".

The prospect will really spin their head to realize that a salesperson is asking them to take some time. This may convince them of your confidence. In addition, you can point out all those things that they may be missing by rejecting the offer.

Chapter 6:

The Art Of Closing The Sale - Without Being A Pushy Or Aggressive Salesman

After a rigorous pre-sales process, closing of a deal should be a walk in the park. The closure should come effortlessly without any tug-of-war between you and prospect. Closure can oscillate towards success as well as failure, depending on the way you handled the deal. Mastering the closure of deals will resolve many hiccups and help you understand how to take advantage of opportunities.

To master the closing of the sale, strategically deal with objections cutting across all the negative tactics and learn how to steer past them victoriously.

Remain attached to the result with a distinctive feeling so that there is no desperation.

Have complete control and conviction over your product to have a grip over your prospect at the time of closure.

The process of closure cannot be isolated as it is incepted right through the first and second phase where trust is established with the prospect and worth of the deal is shared respectively.

Closure comes out to be the last phase that wraps up the whole process.

Closure of a sale should

Carry no confusion or vagueness

Ensure the articulation of terms, rates, clauses and conditions clearly

Realize the prospects concerns and have them addressed.

When to Close

A sale should be closed out of agreement to meet a decision. If the sale is not coming to a conclusion and there are still some problems, as a sales person, you should ease the situation and give the prospect the option of rethinking their decision.

Managing Closure out of Rejection

If you are closing a deal out of rejection, don't ponder over your failure

Keep faith in your sales acumen and talk to yourself positively

\# Don't exaggerate the issue

\# Continue prospecting with better zeal

\# Find a fresh lead and start working over it enthusiastically

How to Close

\# Close the deal on an encouraging note with due respect to mutual decisions.

\# If the prospect agrees to deal offered, take them in a guided way to the closure so that they can be relieved.

\# Have faith in what you are selling to still remain committed and confident.

\# If closure is accompanying rejection, do not get personal. Have faith in yourself and carry a positive attitude

\# Do not leave things unfinished. Take the rejection without aggression, especially if it is in the best interest

\# Sometimes unfinished deals carry enough scope of revival. Don't stop the ticking of your sales-oriented mind and display persistence

\# Keep firm belief in your product as it will show in

your extent of involvement

\# Hone your negotiation skills to make the closing natural

\# Close the deal in a confident and wholehearted manner

Appealing for direct close

Appealing for direct close is always advantageous and uncomplicated. It would save you from many hassles and complexities. A direct request would also appeal to prospects and initiate quick wrapping.

However, quick closure must not be attempted too early lest it may seem abnormal. First, create trust with your prospect and establish rapport.

What to say while closing

Sometimes efficiently and effectively presented sales pitch goes wasted simply because closure was not asked in the first place or not worded properly. As a salesperson, do not take this aspect for granted but actually speak out strategic words.

Some of the sentences and phrases mentioned below can work perfectly well:

"If you sign the contract by tomorrow, we can get the consignment delivered by the end of the week/month"

"Should I start devising the contract to get started with the thing?"

"Would you prefer trying this deal for a week / fortnight / month / quarter?

"If you are find it viable, can we initiate the documentation of the contract?"

"Let's come to a conclusion and start the paperwork"

"Are you all set to take things further?"

"We will book your order on credit so that you can test the grounds"

Conclusion

Becoming a successful salesperson doesn't happen overnight, it will take time and you will have to face a great deal of rejection along the way. You will undoubtedly make mistakes but as long as you learn from them and put that experience into good use, you will eventually become a great salesperson and that belief will further empower your selling abilities.

I will be more than happy to learn how this book has helped you in some way. If you feel you have learned something or you think it offered you some value, please take a moment to leave an honest review on Amazon. It would help many future readers who will be forever grateful to you. As I will!

To Your Success,
Adam Richards

DISCLAIMER AND/OR LEGAL NOTICES:
Every effort has been made to accurately represent this book and it's potential. Results vary with every individual, and your results may or may not be different from those depicted. No promises, guarantees or warranties, whether stated or implied, have been made that you will produce any specific result from this book. Your efforts are individual and unique, and may vary from those shown. Your success depends on your efforts, background and motivation.

The material in this publication is provided for educational and informational purposes. Use of the programs, advice, and information contained in this book is at the sole choice and risk of the reader.

www.ingramcontent.com/pod-product-compliance
Lightning Source LLC
Chambersburg PA
CBHW071235220526
45468CB00002B/862